My Lovely Twin
Story and Coloring Book

Written by Rose Wilson
Illustrated by Frances Espanol

To order additional copies of this book, contact:
Xlibris
1-888-795-4274
www.Xlibris.com
Orders@Xlibris.com

ISBN: Softcover   978-1-7960-5559-7
         EBook   978-1-7960-5558-0

Library of Congress Control Number: 2019912722

Print information available on the last page

Rev. date: 08/30/2019

My Lovely Twin

Story and Coloring Book

Rose Marie helps Beth Ann learn
to ride a tricycle.

Rose Marie and Beth Ann play family with their baby dolls.

Rose Marie serves Beth Ann juice and cookies at a tea party.

Rose Marie and Beth Ann hold hands and walk to the cellar play house.

Rose Marie and Beth Ann
swing high into the sky.

In the Cool of the Country Night.
Whippoorwills whistle while perched on a thistle.
Oak leaves wave as squirrels misbehave.
Baby calves bawl to the mommas' roll call.
Brown bats soar feasting on the bug score.
Bullfrogs ribbit with a bulging throat exhibit.
Lady's eye cream on. See you at dawn.

Rose Wilson

Picturesque Willow
Carved wooden box
Release the two brass locks
Open the hinged cover
Golden chains discover
Grasp with tiny fingers
Coolness in touch lingers
Blue eyes grown big and round
Nana's treasure is found!

Rose Wilson

Life. Death.
Green grass. Brown spot.
Oak tree. Wood porch.
Spotted fawn. Venison meat.
Wedding band. Shriveled hand.
Phone ring. No answer.
New potato. French fries.
White sand. Cement road.
Tight jeans. Tattered knee.
Pearl necklace. Unstrung beads.
New car. Bald tires.
Tooth fairy. False teeth.
Shade tree. Fallen leaves.
Sun rise. Sunset. No regret.

Rose Wilson

Dear Little Playmate,
I'm in a sad state.
Because you're not here,
The dark, I do fear.
Oh, come be with me,
And bring your dolly.
Comfort, your touch lends.
We are jolly friends.
We'll slumber with ease.
Forevermore. Please!

Rose Wilson

Printed in the United States
By Bookmasters